W9-CAV-375

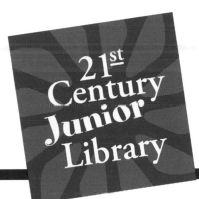

JUPITER

by Ariel Kazunas

CHERRY LAKE PUBLISHING * ANN ARBOR, MICHIGAN

CHERRY
LAKE
Publishing

Published in the United States of America by Cherry Lake Publishing
Ann Arbor, Michigan
www.cherrylakepublishing.com

Content Adviser: Dr. Tobias Owen, University of Hawaii Institute for Astronomy

Photo Credits: Cover and page 4, ©Orlando Florin Rosu/Dreamstime.com,
cover and pages 6, 8, 10, 16, 18, ©NASA; pages12 and 20,
©ASSOCIATED PRESS; page 14, ©Glenda Powers/Dreamstime.com

LIBRARY OF CONGRESS CATALOGING-IN-PUBLICATION DATA
Kazunas, Ariel.
  Jupiter/by Ariel Kazunas.
     p. cm.—(21st century junior library)
  Includes bibliographical references and index.
  ISBN-13: 978-1-61080-086-0 (lib. bdg.)
  ISBN-10: 1-61080-086-9 (lib. bdg.)
  1. Jupiter (Planet)—Juvenile literature. I. Title.
  QB661.K29 2011
  523.45—dc22   2010052613

Cherry Lake Publishing would like to acknowledge the work of
The Partnership for 21st Century Skills.
Please visit www.21stcenturyskills.org for more information.

Printed in the United States of America
Corporate Graphics Inc.
     July 2011
CLFA09

CONTENTS

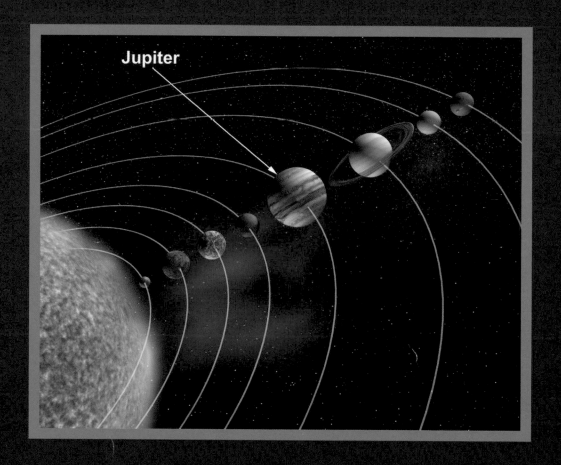

Jupiter

Jupiter is bigger than any other planet in our solar system.

Big and Strong

Jupiter is the largest of the eight planets in our **solar system**. It is twice as big and twice as heavy as all the other planets together.

Jupiter is the fifth planet from the Sun. It travels around the Sun. So do all the other planets.

Astronauts can float in space because gravity is not as strong when they are far away from planets.

Gravity is an invisible force. All objects have gravity. It causes them to pull toward one another. This is what makes the planets move around the Sun. Gravity also keeps us from floating off into space!

Big, heavy objects pull harder than smaller, lighter ones. Jupiter has the strongest gravity of all the planets in our solar system.

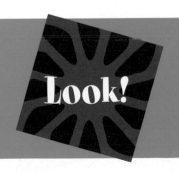

Look!

You can look at your lunch to understand Jupiter's size. Pretend a grapefruit is the Sun. Jupiter would be the size of a cherry. Earth would be as small as a single grain of sugar!

This picture makes it easy to see Jupiter's stripes.

Nowhere to Stand

You could not stand on Jupiter. That's because the planet is made mostly of gases such as hydrogen and helium. Other gases form clouds. Some clouds are white. Others have pale colors. Strong winds blow the clouds around Jupiter. This makes the planet look striped.

The Great Red Spot has been on Jupiter for more than 300 years.

There are huge windstorms inside Jupiter's clouds. One of these storms is called the Great Red Spot. It looks like a giant red swirl on Jupiter's surface.

The Great Red Spot is bigger than Earth. It has been active for hundreds of years.

Create!

Try drawing your own picture of Jupiter. Make sure to include the red and white clouds. Don't forget about the Great Red Spot!

Days and nights go by quickly on Jupiter.

Long Years, Short Days

It takes 12 Earth years for Jupiter to **orbit** the Sun one time. This means a year on Jupiter is 12 times longer than a year on Earth.

Jupiter **rotates** much faster than it orbits. Because of that, a day on Jupiter lasts only 10 hours. That's not even half as long as a day on Earth!

Jupiter spins out like a dancer's skirt.

Jupiter is not perfectly round. This is because it rotates so fast. Think of a ballerina in a skirt. When she spins, her skirt twirls away from her. This makes her look wider. The same thing happens to Jupiter. The planet bulges out in the middle as it spins.

Make a Guess!

What do you think would happen if humans tried to visit Jupiter? Remember that the planet is made of gas. Also remember that it doesn't have the oxygen we need to breathe.

Jupiter might have more moons that haven't been seen yet.

Many Moons

We are used to seeing just one moon in the sky above Earth. Jupiter has at least 63 moons! Four of these moons are much larger than the others. They would be considered planets if they orbited the Sun.

Io's volcanoes leave black and red marks on the moon's surface when they erupt.

One of these moons is called Io. It has more **volcanoes** than any other moon in our solar system.

Another moon is called Ganymede. It is the biggest moon in our solar system.

Callisto is a moon that has been around for a very long time. It has lots of **craters** from being hit by other objects in space.

Think!

Did you know there are rings around Jupiter? They weren't discovered until 1979. This was a long time after Jupiter was first discovered. Why do you think it took so long for anyone to notice the rings?

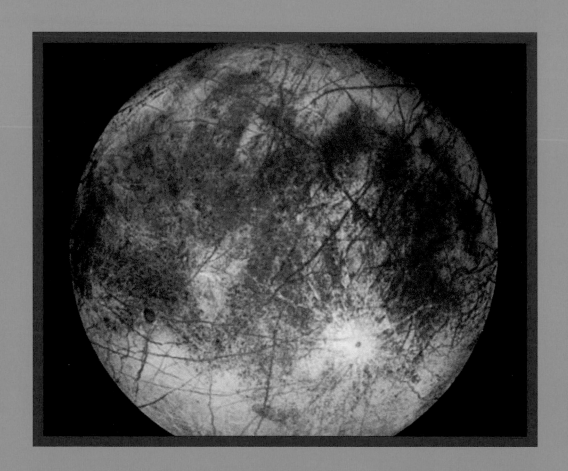

The surface of Europa is covered with patches of
ice and iceberg-like objects.

Europa is Jupiter's other big moon. It is covered in ice. It also has a solid **core**. **Scientists** think there may be a saltwater ocean between the ice and the core. There could be life in this ocean!

Jupiter is very different from Earth. Scientists continue to study it for new clues about our solar system. What will they find out next?

GLOSSARY

core (KOR) center part of a planet

craters (KRAY-turz) holes caused by one object in space hitting other

gravity (GRAV-uh-tee) the invisible force between objects in space that makes them pull on each other

orbit (OR-bit) to travel in a path around a central point

rotates (ROH-tates) spins

solar system (SOH-lur SISS-tuhm) a star, such as the Sun, and all the planets and moons that move around it

scientists (SYE-uhn-tissts) people who study nature and make discoveries

volcanoes (vol-KAY-nohz) mountains that throw out smoke, lava, and ashes from vents in the top

FIND OUT MORE

BOOKS

Aguilar, David A. *11 Planets: A New View of the Solar System*. Washington, DC: National Geographic Society, 2008.

Hansen, Rosanna. *Jupiter*. Minneapolis: Lerner Publications Co., 2010.

Landau, Elaine. *Jupiter*. New York: Children's Press, 2008.

WEB SITES

HubbleSite: Gallery
hubblesite.org/gallery
A great place to see fun pictures of outer space!

NASA: Solar System Exploration
solarsystem.nasa.gov/kids
Check out these fun activities from NASA.

Space.com—Our Solar System: Facts, Formation and Discovery
www.space.com/solarsystem/
Learn more about the objects in our solar system and how they were formed.

INDEX

ABOUT THE AUTHOR

Ariel Kazunas lives on the Oregon coast, writing books for kids and working at the Sitka Center for Art and Ecology. She has also worked for several nonprofit magazines. Ariel loves exploring our planet—especially by hand, foot, bike, and boat—and camping out under the stars.